the nail
style book
by the untouchables

Beauty & Health Publishing Ltd

To Bob, my husband and friend, without whose love, support and sense of humour, this project would have been a lot harder.
– *Jacqui Jefford*

To my friends, family and clients who have supported me throughout my career and allowed me to experiment using my creativity. Special thanks to Jacqui, my partner and friend whose joint creativity in this venture has helped to make this book and partnership so special.
– *Sue Marsh*

A special thank you also goes to all the fashion designers who helped launch nails onto the catwalk, all the designers and make-up artists with whom we have worked during London Fashion Week and *Nails Plus* magazine for believing in us.
– *Sue Marsh & Jacqui Jefford*

First published in Great Britain in 2001
by Beauty & Health Publishing Ltd
Alexander House
Forehill, Ely
Cambs CB7 4ZA
00 44 (0)1353 66 55 77

ISBN: 0-9541268-0-7

BEAUTY & HEALTH PUBLISHING LTD

Mel B by Sue Marsh

contents

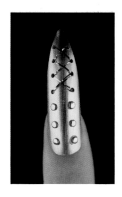

Introduction

Ever since we started working in the media and fashion world we've realised that make-up and hair artists have material they can refer to for inspiration. However, this was and is not the case for us, as the nails industry is still in its infancy and as such, has no real history to refer back to. Only in the last five years have magazines, newspapers, stylists, designers and photographers become fully aware of the existence of specialist nail professionals – artists in their own right. We believe that nail technicians should also be employed to work on fashion shoots that involve the exposure of fingernails, instead of leaving it to the make-up artist, who has historically applied the polish. We are the professionals in this field – we understand the procedures and are trained to do the job.

Through our work with *Nails Plus* magazine we've realised that other technicians feel the same way. There is a sad lack of motivational photographic images and styles brought together in one inspirational volume to be used as a reference manual highlighting techniques on natural nails, enhancements, flat nail art or 3D work. As education is a subject we both feel passionately about, we've realised that there is a need to produce a series of books to inspire technicians wishing to embark on a career in photographic and fashion work. These books will present ideas on how to use various skills and methods so that technicians can design their own personal stunning artwork.

We thank the team at *Nails Plus* for allowing us to create many of its front cover images and giving us complete artistic license in their creation. It is very rare in any photographic media work that you can design whatever inspires your creative talent, more often than not the photographer and artistic director already have the style-idea and know what they want. So to be able to let our imaginations run wild and see the results in print, has been a great opportunity.

We hope you find this book inspirational and that for those that want to, it will allow you to take your nail skills to a new level. This first UK Nail Style Book is about imagination and creativity. Not everyone will understand every picture – we all see things differently – however we hope that the designs will intrigue you and have you questioning and experimenting with your products. Both of us adore our work whether we are working on a client in the salon, on a photo shoot or backstage at a fashion show; it is a privilege to be in an industry where so many people feel passionate about their work. We are all artists at heart because when we perform nail treatments, we are working on a canvas producing a piece of beauty, creating art. We hope you enjoy the designs we have chosen in this publication and that it does inspire you to pick up your brush and try something a little different.

Jacqui Jefford & Sue Marsh
The Untouchables

Jacqui Jefford

I had my first set of nails applied when I was sixteen years old in the Dorchester Hotel, London. I was hooked for life.

When I met my husband Bob, he whisked me off to the depths of Wales where I could only find sheep but no nail technician to do my nails. So I took a course with my then nail technician, Janet Thomas. I then took a six week apprenticeship in nails, which was unheard of in those days!

In Wales I did my own nails but was constantly badgered by those around me to do their nails. So began my long career in nails. I worked from home for the first five years and had my babies in between. Chantal was born at home so I was working through my contractions! Then with the advent of four children, two under three years old, I decided to get a nanny and a nail desk in a hair salon. I became so busy and decided to teach. I went to college and took Beauty Therapy Levels II and III and began teaching at Salisbury College and Morley College, London. I taught for Cosmic Nails for a year and Florida Nails for another year. I began to love education so much that I became an NVQ assessor and approached Creative Nail Design to become one of its educators.

My qualifications portfolio is quite varied, I have trained with Creative Nail Design, LCN UK, Cosmic Nails, OPI, The Nail Place and Janet Thomas.

To date I am part of the Elite International Team Creative and an NVQ assessor and internal verifier for ANT (Association of Nail Technicians).

My current passion, alongside the running of my salon in Salisbury, is as the scheme co-ordinator and founder of the ANT Satellite Assessment Centres and advisor to local colleges and training organisations on all educational issues within the nails industry. I am also proud to have been involved in numerous nail-related publications on education, nail technology, nail style as well as codes of practice and an NVQ assessor's handbook.

Sue Marsh

I entered the nails industry by default about sixteen years ago. I was working in a boutique and was unable to afford to have my nails enhanced. Luckily a colleague working in the same building as me was a nail technician. She taught me all her nail skills, sculpting liquid & powder, gels and fibreglass nails, and then handed me a job. I worked alongside her for a year and then decided to go it alone.

My first nail salon was a small holding in Carterton, Oxon. After a year I moved to Swindon and opened a nail salon there. Those early days were very busy as I made the decision to open a second salon in Burford, Oxon, whilst progressing with the Swindon business. These two I ran simultaneously for five years.

My next move was to London where I joined The Nail Place in Oxford Street as an educator. Eighteen months later I was bored with London so I packed up and made a bee-line for Malta. In Malta I earned my living through nail services. It was during my time in Malta that I realised and developed my creative potential as I had time to spend producing unusual nail designs such as the freehand painted Geisha girl that I am now well known for.

I came back to England to get married. I worked in various salons on and off but spent the majority of my time teaching nail skills. In order to progress myself and keep abreast of the changing trends I took an NVQ in 1995. It was at this time I became even more interested in the emerging nails industry and technicians and took a more proactive approach to the industry.

Untouchables

The Untouchables

It was in 1995 through teaching that we met. We were both very keen on education and teaching nail skills. We immediately became friends, recognising in one another a passion for nail artistry and each impressed with the other's drive, passion, motivation, skills and inspiring persona.

We met occasionally over the next year and spent time together in London whenever a teaching commitment afforded the excursion.

Education has always been a passion for both of us, as we understood that education is the key to becoming a first class nail technician. So we had an early vision which had yet to be realised and come to fruition.

At the time we both concurrently built our careers: Sue working progressively in the media and building up her private celebrity client list and Jacqui absorbing herself in her own salon business and building a reputation within nail education.

It was in these early days together that we were asked by a top UK make-up artist, Val Garland, one of Sue's clients, whether we could help out at London

Fashion Week. The show happened to be for the designer, Fabio Piraz, and is one that we'll never forget. We were asked to design nails that had previously been just figments of our imaginations. At last we had been given the artistic opportunity to design our own-style nails to the look of the make-up, hair and clothes – so we literally went wild. The theme was Dominatrix – so we produced nails that turned men's faces white with fright. The corkscrews, the chain mail, the barbed wire and the cut-outs were all very aggressive.

We worked for over three weeks making twenty-two sets of nails for London Fashion Week and spent a fortune on materials. When the day of Fabio's show came the models went crazy; they loved it, they had never seen or worn anything like it before. When they went out onto the catwalk they really played up to the cameras with their hands and later all said that their nails made them feel powerful yet playful. The Press also went wild over the nails and consequently the following week saw us exposed in most national newspapers and Sunday supplements. The demand for our work was coming in thick and fast so we decided

an agent was the best way to manage our time and work effectively. This was the beginning of The Untouchables – we have since become so busy that we've turned our success into a new venture and now run our own agency and share the workload with other first class technicians. It was this first London Fashion Week that inspired the name 'Untouchables'. It referred directly to the nails we had produced as the models could wear them, but couldn't touch anything, they were simply gimmicks.

Our work is varied, sometimes very time consuming and poorly paid, but we love all of it. We meet very interesting people, sometimes get to see beautiful locations and most of all do the work that we love the most – nails! We are a team in every sense of the word – loyal to one another and fully aware of each other's strengths and weaknesses – and we work these to our advantage.

The Untouchables team currently houses eight professionals: Sue and Jacqui as its nail art and design directors, Jane Cook, Liesl Silcock, Debbie Easter, Marianne Manley and Chrissy Con as its nail professionals and Michelle Hardy as booking director and co-ordinator.

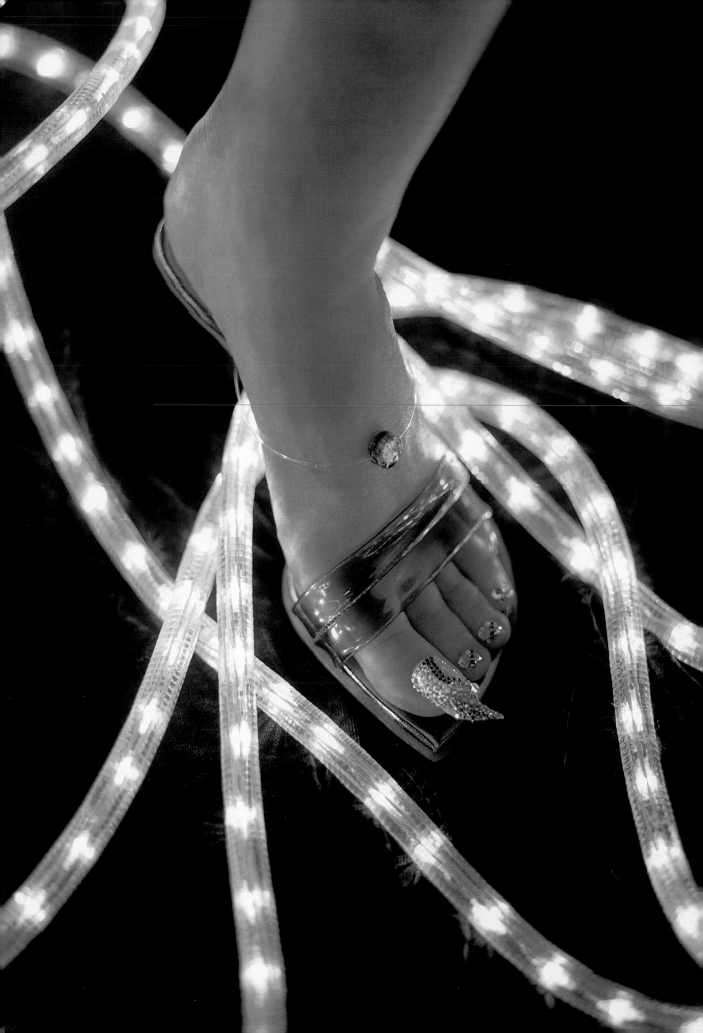

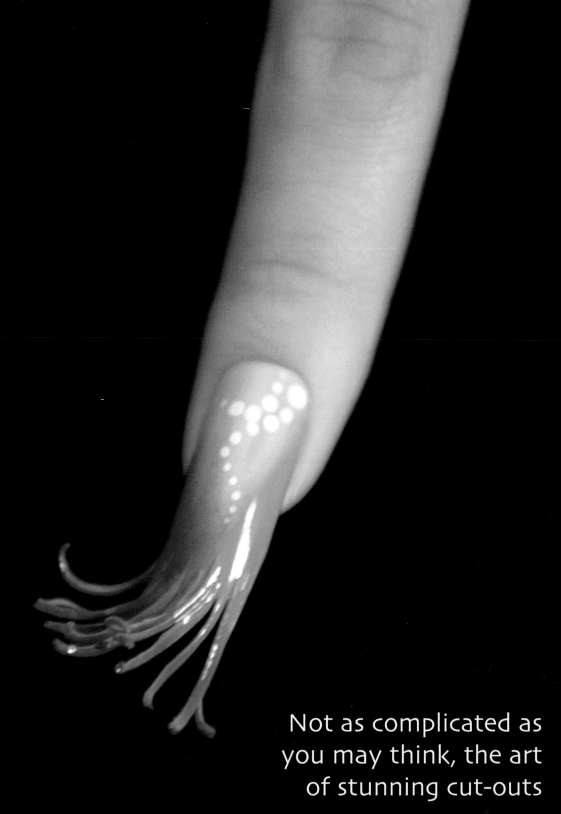

Not as complicated as you may think, the art of stunning cut-outs

Sea anemone

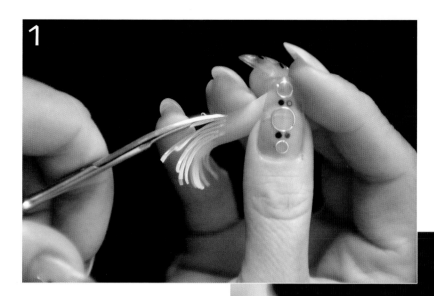

Step 1

With sharp curved scissors, cut into the free edge of tip and strips of plastic will peel back in curves.

Step 2

Using an airbrush on the top side of the nail, spray pink paint all over the tip.

Step 3

On the underside of the nail, airbrush using turquoise colour. Follow to top side and touch up the free edge.

Step 4

On top side using a marbelling tool and white acrylic paint, dab on dots from large to small in an uneven line.

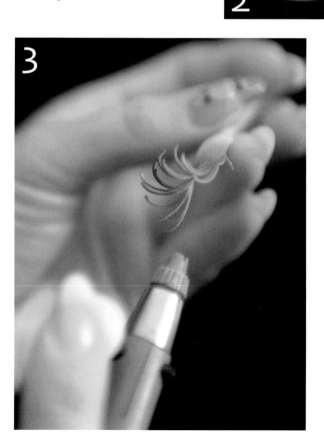

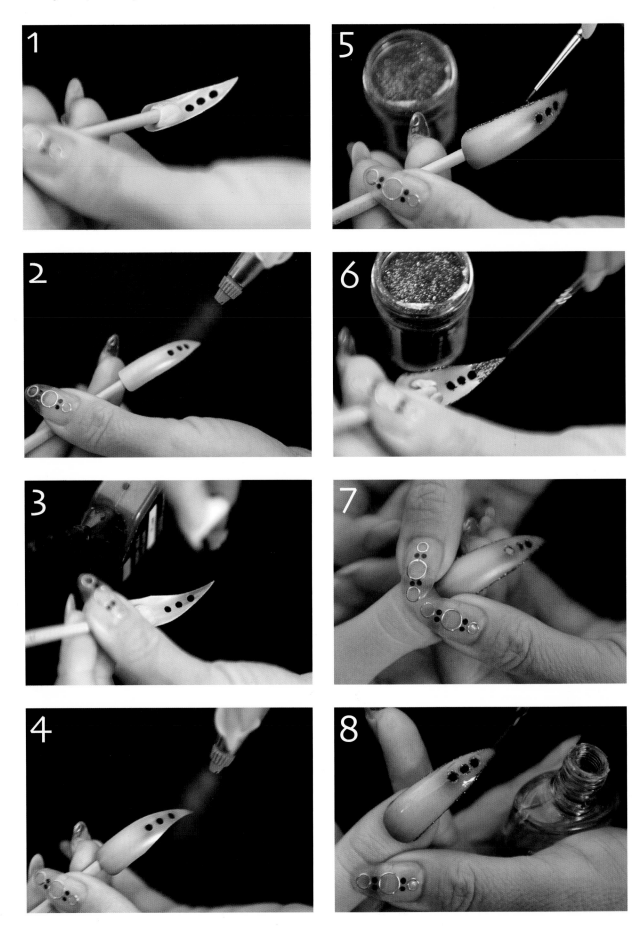

Spearhead

Combining cut-out techniques with airbrush and glitter styling

Step 1
Use a long curved tip. Attach tip to cuticle stick with Blu-Tack. Make three holes down the centre of nail tip using a drill.

Step 2
Using airbrush spray coat the base with yellow colour on the full length of the tip.

Step 3
Spray underside of free edge on tip in bronze. (Always remember to paint the flip side of the nail as movement in photographs catches this detail).

Step 4
Using an orange stick catch the cuticle area of tip and free edge, and then lowlight with bronze to give depth.

Step 5
Using small brush dip into top coat, and then with wet brush pick up traces of bronze glitter and touch up edges of holes and outside edges of nail tip.

Step 6
Remember flip side and add glitter to this area using a small nail art brush.

Step 7
Attach nail design to finger.

Step 8
Using top coat seal colour.

London
Fashion
Week

We started getting involved behind the scenes of London Fashion Week (LFW) about five years ago. Before that, the only knowledge we had of the event was from snippets on TV or through magazines and newspapers.

It is a very expensive event for us, as we have never been paid for any work, materials or travel, however it is made well worth it by the sheer excitement and being part of a large team that is designing a whole new look for the fashion industry.

Once at the show, it is nearly always the make-up artist that we liaise with, as the nail colours usually match the make-up being worn on a particular catwalk presentation. If we are lucky, we sometimes get to meet the hair and make-up artists before the show to discuss various looks, but more often than not we find ourselves embarking on a few frantic phone calls 24 hours beforehand to decide upon the polish colours to be used. It is rare that we know what shows and how many shows we will be involved in even four or five days before London Fashion Week opens. In most cases it is just one or two days before the event that we get a call-out. In fact, LFW is so frantic and born of disarray that there are times when we're called to a show which directly follows the one we are currently working on.

For this reason it is critical that we carry a full working kit at all times. This includes manicure and pedicure implements and products as well as a full spectrum of nail polishes. We currently hold around 250 different polish colours in our kits. The only time we ever need to use nail enhancement products is when we need to apply a tip to a model missing the odd fingernail. We never apply nail extensions, everything is done on the natural nail as there is not enough time for application procedures and of course the model is left without the knowledge of how to or where to go for maintenance.

Dress code for the show is simple – never dress up, always dress down. If you look like you've just walked off a catwalk yourself, you are seen as very odd. We find that when you're crawling around on the floor polishing toe nails (Sue's job as Jacqui cannot fit into tight spaces!) it doesn't pay to be wearing your favourite Gucci trousers. You need to be adaptable to any situation and circumstance, so high heels and tight skirts are just not appropriate. Backstage is very stressful, especially towards showtime with designers, stylists, make-up and hair artists all battling against time to get the models ready. It is very unlikely that any show ever starts on time – we always make sure we have allowed for this before promising to be with the next. Now we have extended The Untouchables team it is much easier to balance the work between shows.

In the bigger shows like Givenchy, McQueen, Tristan Webber and Marcus Luptfer top models are used, so we make a list of all the models we need to paint, and then check that everyone has been buffed, oiled and polished before showtime. Whenever we have been asked to do anything really wacky we have prepared the nails well beforehand and just attached them before the show starts and likewise removed them as soon as the model steps off the stage. Some nails we've made, such as barbed wire and corkscrews, have been so intricate and fiddly that we've had to take the models to the toilet as they cannot touch anything for fear of damaging themselves or the nails!

Backstage is much more exciting than sitting out at the front watching the show. The atmosphere is always electric and there's never a dull moment. We now meet the same people year after year, which is great for our reputation and means that repeat work not only comes from a job well done, but also the people we have met and built relationships with. The models are really great to work with and we always give them good, sound advice on caring for their nails whilst we are working on them. One of the first things we noticed back at the beginning, was the amount of damage on the model's fingernails from stick-on nails that had been used for previous shows due to the lack of the make-up artist's nail knowledge. We quickly devised a way of using tips without applying them to the natural nail and being able to pop them off without damaging the model's natural nail plate. When you think how many shows these girls do in one London Fashion week, and let's not forget Paris, Milan and New York, it's not surprising their nails are shabby to say the least! We have built a good sound relationship with a lot of the models who know that we care about their nails and some have even proudly displayed beautifully groomed fingernails to us six months after taking our advice.

Lastly, it is so exciting to be able to stretch our artistic abilities to the limit when working with certain designers such as Alexander McQueen. Some designers have allowed us artistic licence to do what we want with the nails, in other words we have been designing nails to match designer clothing. However, it is still very satisfying to work with the designers who prefer the natural look because their clothes need to be complemented with understated, elegant yet beautiful nails, and let's face it, there is nothing more beautiful than a perfectly groomed set of natural nails. We now have a team of five very highly qualified technicians who work with us on photo shoots and back stage at London Fashion week, and as each year goes by the team gets ever bigger.

Bug's life

Using a combination of liquid & powder, fibreglass and freezer bag ties – build a 3D dragon fly

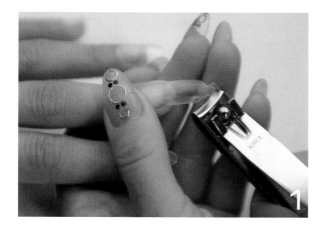

Step 1

Apply crystal clear tip to middle finger. Leave a long free edge, approximately 3¼" over finger tip. Using tip snippers cut triangular shape into tip. Leave a diamond shape at point of tip to build head of bug on.

Step 2

Cut tip either side of edge below diamond shape, but don't cut off diamond.

Step 3

Lift up two free pieces of cut tip behind head to produce antennae.

Step 4

Using white powder (you need this to see detail when using crystal tip), pick up a small bead to build up diamond area into 3D bug's head.

Step 5

Apply two tiny balls of liquid & powder to antennae to give image of bug-like features.

Step 6

Now start to build segments behind head.

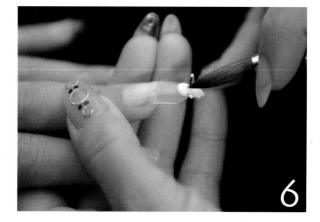

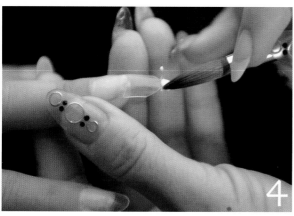

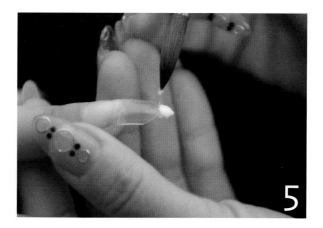

step-by-step

Step 7
To get more detail while liquid & powder is still not set, use a chisel to carve gap between bug head and segment.

Step 8
Continue backwards towards cuticle to build body with small liquid & powder beads. Taper last bead on nail plate making it smaller as it moves up to the cuticle.

Step 9
Strip paper off outside of freezer bag ties! Bend into wing shape of bug, use two and twist together.

Step 10
Push middle section of wings into ridge between section two and three of bug.

Step 11
Seal wings between second and third section with bead of liquid & powder, and hold for approximately three minutes until product hardens.

Step 12
Paint bug silver or any colour of your choice.

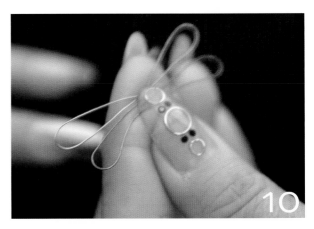

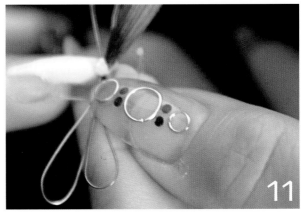

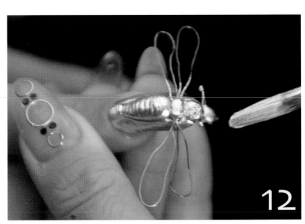

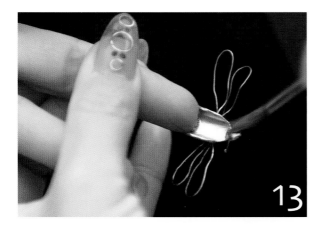

Step 13
Paint the underside of the bug.

Step 14
Cut fibreglass strip. Peel off from adhesive paper and re-adhere onto free edge, avoid touching fibreglass with fingers wherever possible.

Step 15
Use fibreglass for bug wings. Attach it to the underside of wings. Fibreglass looks like delicate wings of a dragonfly!

Step 16
Cut around wings to remove surplus fibreglass and then the wings are finished. Do not use adhesives.

Step 1a
Using clear liquid & powder place bead in cuticle area (zone 3).

Step 2a
Using stripped freezer bag wire, place onto bead and allow to set diagonally across nail plate towards free edge.

Step 3a
Continue until you build up three diagonal strips of wire across the nail plate, using acrylic to set it all in place.

Step 4a
Twist the three wires together and trim with a wire cutter to get the effect of a crysalis. Leave 6mm of wire and bend back onto the nail tip.

Step 5a
Finally when you have set all three wires onto the nail, go over the surface of the nail with liquid & powder and embed the wire into the product.

Step 6a
When you have finished all the embedding on the fingers and thumb, twist the loose wire on the free edge and cut with wire cutters ¼" above the free edge. Twist and turn back onto the top side of the nail, to look like a tail.

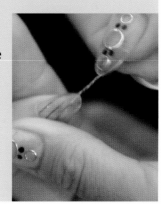

Photographic nails

We have spent nearly five years attending photo shoots and in that time have found it is rare that we're given the opportunity of injecting our own ideas regarding the artistic portrayal of hands and nails. It has been quite an uphill struggle trying to convince and show stylists and photographers that nail technicians have artistic skills as well as technical ability. However, it seems we are finally getting there!

Performing nail treatments or nail artwork for a photographic shoot is very different from any other type of work a nail technician executes. The nearest thing to it is competition nail work. Why? Because the detail has to be so exact. Any slight glitch in the polish application and the camera will magnify it many times over. And the photographer will pick up any minute in-consistencies the second he/she looks through the lens.

Photographic work is not for the faint hearted or sensitive soul. When commissioned to do a job, a nail technician may be asked to change a particular look many times before the photographer finds what he/she is looking for through the lens. For anyone who has ever been behind a camera, you will know that what you see with the naked eye is very different to the framed shot viewed through a lens and it is the photographer's expertise which intuitively knows whether a shot is going to work or not.

When on a shoot we always carry a full nail, hand and foot kit. This includes manicure and pedicure implements, nail enhancement products and a full range of polishes and nail art. Unlike working on fashion shows, we generally know in advance what is expected of us and which colours will be needed. In some cases the stylist provides the colours on the day, however we always carry back-up in case of problems. We have been on many a shoot for a cosmetic company and ended up using another company's polishes for one reason or another.

Most of our work to date has really been just basic manicures and pedicures. Although on some occasions a magazine will be writing about nail trends or producing a nail art step-by-step feature and need illustrations. We have found that building a good rapport with beauty editors can open many doors as they do approach us for quotes on a whole range of nail issues, and it is a really lovely feeling to be recognised as a professional in your own right.

We recommend, if you decide to take up this specialist career route, that you be prepared to sit around for hours on end in a studio. It's not a whole heap of fun, however it can be very interesting and insightful to watch the make-up artists, hair stylists and the photographers at work. Another great aspect to this work is the amount of interesting people you'll meet – as well as the food you'll consume on the job!

Photo shoots have a habit of running well over the time allocated, as a multitude of things can and do hold things up. So we've learnt to never make any plans as we may well still be in the studio at 11pm. When on location we are often out and about in all weather, which can be fun when it's fine, but is downright awful when it's cold and wet.

We always carry a list of industry contacts when out on a shoot, so if we find we're missing a particular product we are able to call it in and get it sent over immediately by taxi. We have found that on a few occasions we have had to ring London salons to beg, borrow or steal nail products that the photographer has requested at the last minute.

If you decide that photographic work is the path you wish to pursue, then take time to practice at home with your camera. Get a feel for what does and doesn't work in a shot. Experiment with different angles to show off your nail designs to perfection. Keep a folder of your artwork so that potential clients can see what you're capable of and remember, what you don't like, someone else will – so carry everything. Be technical and precise. The polish line around a cuticle should be perfect, your nail art should be precise – attention to detail is paramount in this business. If you do a thorough job then you will get repeat work, but do a sloppy job and all you will get is a bad reputation.

Do not expect to earn a fortune at the beginning. We didn't start to earn any money until we had been working for around two years. It's all about building up a good reputation, founded on trust and capability. You will find the more high-profile the job, the less you'll be paid if anything! However it is these jobs that are so important to your portfolio.

It goes without saying when we've organised a shoot that we always choose a model with beautiful hands and nails. We also spend a lot of time considering the background and various props we will be needing. If it's a facial shot then we make sure that hair stylists and make-up artists are booked and that the model is ready to go when the photographer arrives. A photographer's time is precious and costly, so it doesn't pay to waste it. We have often found that to cut time to a minimum on the day, if we know the model well, we perform the manicure on the previous day. And when we use stick-on tips the artwork is created well in advance. If we know that we have a shoot that will involve something very complicated, we create the nails weeks beforehand as some nails, such as the set of corkscrews above, can take up to twenty hours to make.

Just remember – be passionate about your work and people will be inspired by you. Never take no for an answer and always stretch your artistic abilities to the limit.

be passionate about your work and people will be inspired by you

Jet stream

Black powder with
clear tips and
rhinestones for
dazzling effects

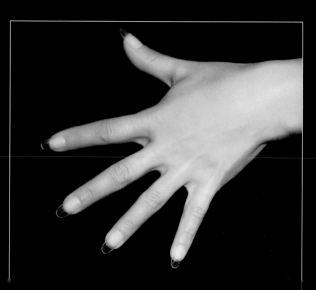

Tip application

Step 1
Prepare nail plate for tip adhesive.

Step 2
Place bead of adhesive in well area of tip.

Step 3
Using nail clipper, cut tip to required length.

Step 4
Using tip cutters cut out an angle to produce an oval shape.

Step 5
File tip with nail file to even shape and tidy the edges.

Step 6
Tips on all fingers and thumb are all preshaped and prepared.

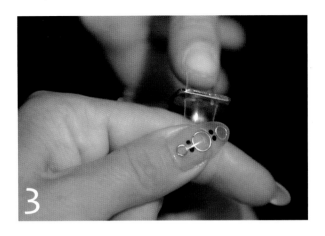

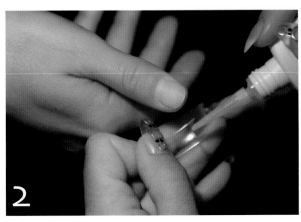

Thumb

Step 1
Using liquid & black powder the design for the thumb nail is sculptured onto the clear tip.

Step 2
Using liquid & black powder, follow outside shape of tip with design leaving point in the top centre.

Step 3
Follow both sides of tip using liquid & black powder.

Step 4
Black powder is sculptured in at the cuticle to point up towards the free edge design.

Step 5
Using brush with clear powder, pick up black jet rhinestones to place in line from tip to point in cuticle.

Step 6
This shot shows what the jets look like going towards the cuticle.

Step 7
Using jets around one side of the cuticle, stab the design.

Step 8
Using small beads of liquid & powder, slowly cover your design and allow to set. Buff and shine to finish.

TOP TIPS

• *A clear bead of liquid & powder can be used to seal back.*
• *Try out various coloured powders and matching rhinestones.*

Forefinger

Step 1
Apply liquid & black powder bead to right side of tip.

Step 2
Press diagonal line from right side of free edge across and up half of the left side of the free edge.

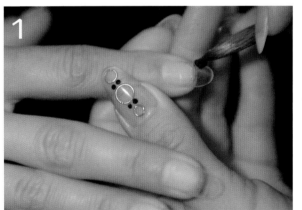

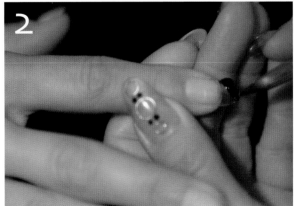

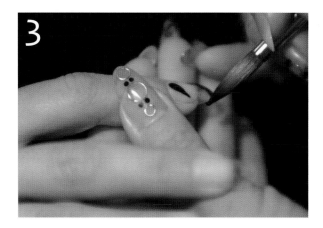

Step 3
From bottom right-hand side of cuticle, apply small bead of liquid & black powder and roll towards left side.

Step 4
Pick up jet rhinestone with brush and place at point of arrow.

Step 5
Using your brush to pick up rhinestones, place each one carefully under diagonal design on free edge keeping the same distance between the stones for continuity.

Step 6
Using pink powder, place beads from tip to cuticle and cover entire nail with product until all design on nail is embedded and the surface feels smooth to touch.

Middle finger

Step 1
Place liquid & black powder on free edge and begin to press product into the shape of a sharp edged triangle, the point being in the middle where the tip meets with the natural nail and the wider area of the triangle stretches to the outer free edge.

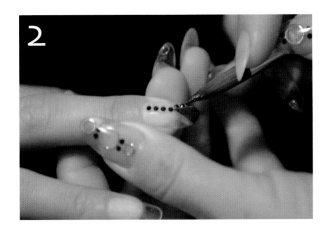

Step 1
Place liquid & black powder on free edge and begin to press and pull product from left to right.

Step 2
Build a smile line on seam of stress area to produce French-style free edge.

Step 3
Place small bead of liquid & pink powder to secure design. Pick up black jet rhinestone and begin to place jets around the cuticle and up the side walls of the nail up to the free edge.

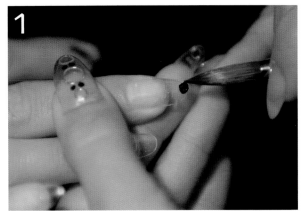

Step 2
From the cuticle, place small bead of pink powder to secure black jet rhinestones. Place jets from cuticle up to point of liquid & black powder. Continue either side of the triangle.

Step 3
Using pink powder, place beads over jets and triangle design. Buff and shine

Third finger

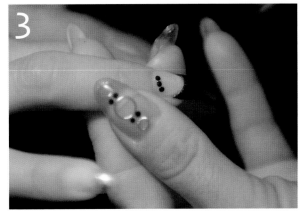

Step 4
Continue to fill the nail plate in jet rhinestones using your brush and flow with the crescent shape.

Step 5
Gradually the nail plate is filled and the crescent gets smaller.

Step 6
Once nail plate is full of jet rhinestones pick up bead of clear liquid & powder and cover jets, press and pull to free edge.

Step 7
Apply final bead to nail to finish. Buff to high shine.

Little finger

Step 1
Place black powder bead in cuticle area, gently pull bead and roll back up towards smile line.

Step 2
The shape you are trying to achieve looks like a stretched triangle.

Step 3
Using another small bead of black powder, start at point of triangle and press outwards to free edge of tip, leaving triangular points in the centre of the smile line.

Step 4
This design should look like a neck tie.

Step 5

Use black rhinestones to fill in the free edge area. Use your brush to pick them up, and space them out leaving a small gap between each one.

Step 6

Using pink powder, apply a small bead and place jet rhinestones in the area on the free edge.

Step 7

To finish, place small beads of pink powder from tip to cuticle and cover entire nail with product until the whole design is embedded and smooth. Buff and shine.

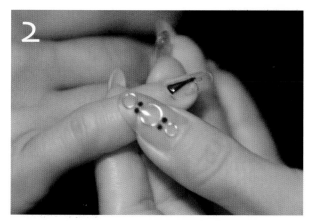

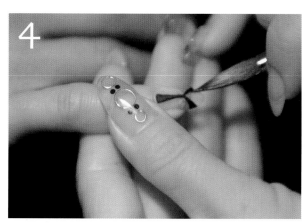

Nails Plus magazine

Back in December 1997 the first ever issue of *Nails Plus* magazine was born. It was the first nails-only related business-to-business publication to be produced for the UK nails industry, and as such it was embraced wholeheartedly and with much enthusiasm. However this may not have been the case without the creative injection it received from The Untouchables.

To produce a successful publication to a small market such as the nails industry is a tall order. It was clear that *Nails Plus* needed to be informative, communicative, educational and most importantly, visually outstanding. The Untouchables were the answer. At the time, the *Nails Plus* publisher Julie Day was a client of Sue Marsh and so the seed was born. Keen to see a stand-alone nails publication, it didn't take much in the way of persuasion to include the skills of The Untouchables at this crucial stage of the proceedings. The front covers needed to be stylish, punchy, imaginative, innovative, topical and fashion-led. The Untouchables had all the answers and more. And so began a fruitful and to date, inseparable relationship.

The first year of *Nails Plus* was a nail-biting experience for all involved. Would it take off? Would it be a success? Would it have the impact necessary to see it survive? The answers were yes, yes and yes! The team at *Nails Plus* could see the individual talents and skills of both Jacqui and Sue and was keen to make the most of this fount of knowledge and expertise. The Untouchables were given *carte blanche* and asked to create artistically challenging front covers. This they accomplished with ease and style. This relationship was not just to *Nails Plus'* advantage however, The Untouchables were more than pleased to have an outlet to express their inner creativity and expose their artistic abilities to a wider audience.

The early success of *Nails Plus* can partly be attributed to the tireless work of The Untouchables. The UK nails industry was crawling around in the dark, without focus or strong

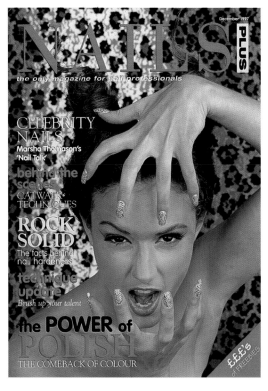

direction. The magazine gave nail technicians and manicurists a port of call – somewhere they could find inspiration and information. And what made the publication so spell-binding was its front covers. Technicians up and down the country wanted to know how to create the nails conceived by The Untouchables. Never before had such imaginative designs been seen, in fact there was a dire lack of visually stunning nail images in the UK. At last this niche had been filled.

As time has moved on and *Nails Plus* remains the leading UK nails-only trade title, its relationship with The Untouchables has blossomed and become ever closer. Not just nail-design innovators and creators, Jacqui and Sue also inject valuable information and advice to the publication acting as consultants and columnists on various issues from education, health and safety procedures, chemical issues, technical data, techniques and applications, as well as offering consistently high quality imagery.

It's a marriage made in heaven and one that continues to grow and evolve alongside the UK nails industry. In Jacqui and Sue, *Nails Plus* has found an invaluable combination of creativity, technical ability, educational skill and most of all, two poetic personalities.

Alex Fox

Alex Fox
editor

Acknowledgements

All nails by The Untouchables

Photography:
Page 8, 12, 13, 14, 16, 18, 20, 25, 28, 36, 37, 41 – James Cumpsty
Page 1, 7, 24, 42 – Richard Ecclestone
Page 5 (Boy George) – karlgrant.co.uk@eminent (shot for Attitude magazine 2000)

Editor: Alex Fox
Marketing: Julie Day
Designer: Deborah Day
Production: Andrew Pennington & Ben Watson

Cover: sponsored by Swarovski

SWAROVSKI
C O M P O N E N T S

Models: Kim Wrigley, Kelly Bignell, Samantha Aitken, Susie Langhorn, Katherine Popplestone, Justine Case, Danielle Parkinson

Make-up: Claudine
Hair: Claire, Tony & Guy, Salisbury
Shoes: Juliana, Due Passe

Products: Kiss UK, Designer Nails, Creative Nail Design, K-Sa-Ra

Nail technicians: Liesl Silcock

Special thanks to:
Val Garland, Karen at Blunt, Wear & Tear, Smitten, Swarvoski, Boy George, Mel B, Sharlene Spiteri, Jim Thompson at Oriental Restaurant/Bar, Rachel at Streeters, Attitude Magazine

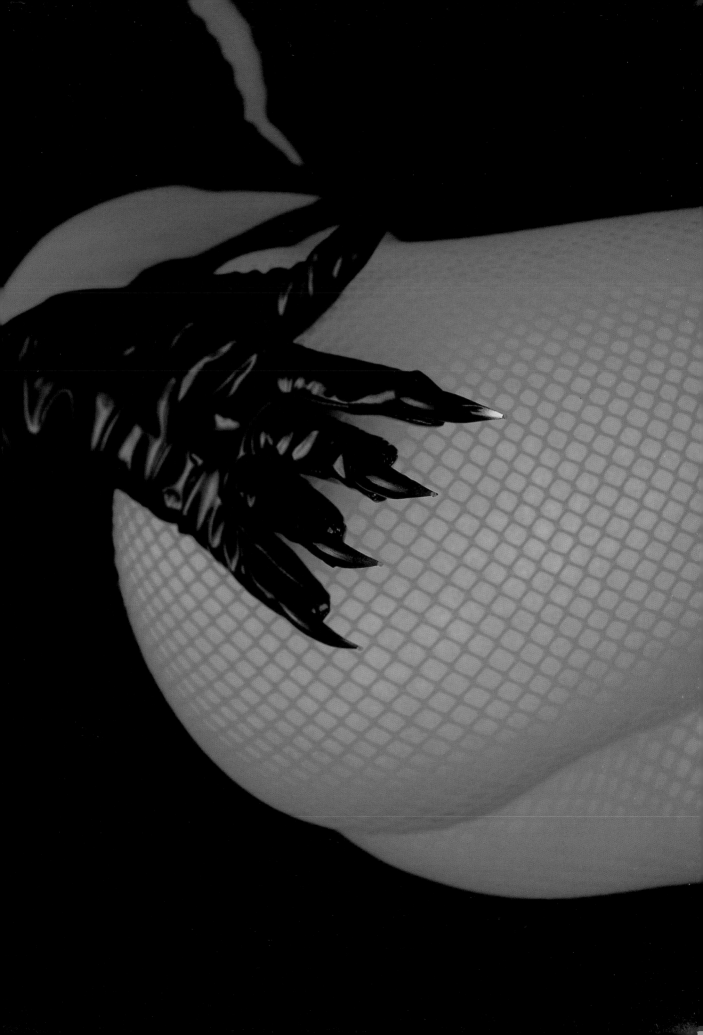

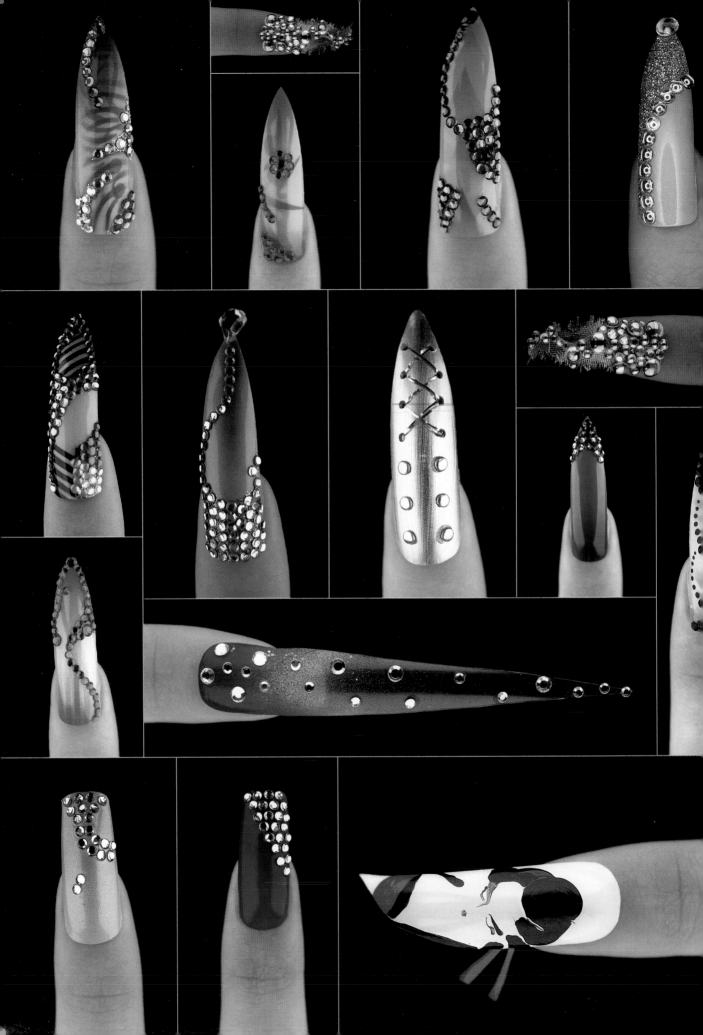